All in

written by Jeremy Strong
illustrated by Steve Smallman

Chapter One
Something Special

The friends were playing on the swings in the park. Jojo stood on her seat and began to swing backwards and forwards.

"I'm flying!"

Ben stood on his seat too.

"I can fly higher!" he shouted.

"Come on Mouse!" yelled Jojo. "Why don't you have a go?" But Mouse didn't want to stand on a swing. He felt a lot safer on the ground. Before the others could say any more there was a loud shout from behind them.

"Hey! You children! Get down! Swings are for sitting on!"

It was Grumpyboots, taking his little dog Scrap for a walk. Ben and Jojo quickly sat down.

"I didn't see him creep up on us," Jojo muttered. "The old spoil sport."

"Let's go to the secret room," suggested Sam. "He can't see us there."

As they set off for the castle, Donut came running towards them.

"Hello!" he grinned. "What are you lot up to?"

"We're hiding from Grumpyboots," said Ben, pointing to the old man.

"We're going to the secret room," said Sam.

The others looked at her. Donut had not been friends with them for very long. They hadn't told him about the secret room. Donut was all ears. "The secret room? What's that?" he asked.

Ben frowned. "It's our secret place. We'll show you, but you must not tell anyone."

Mouse suddenly butted in. "Yes, but we'll only show you if you bring something special for the room."

"Good idea, Mouse," Ben agreed. "You bring something special back this afternoon, Donut. Then we'll show you the secret room."

Donut scratched his head. "What sort of special?" he asked.

"Very special," Mouse said firmly.

"Right," said Donut, and he went racing off.

The others watched him go.

"I wonder what he'll bring?" said Mouse.

Chapter Two

A Special Secret

Donut searched his house from top to bottom.
His little sister Cleo followed him and asked what he was doing.

"It's a secret."

Cleo wanted to know what the secret was.

"I'm not telling you," said Donut.

Cleo began to pester her big brother more and more.

"All right, listen." Donut whispered in her ear.

Cleo jumped up and down.

"I am not a Niggly Nagbag!" she yelled, and she ran off shouting. "Mum! Mum! Duncan says I'm a Niggly Nagbag! I'm not, am I? Tell him, Mum."

But Donut was not listening to her any longer. He had seen something special. He had seen something **very**, **VERY** special.

Donut found an old sheet.

He carefully placed it over his gift

for the secret room and set off for the park.

Donut met the friends in the park.
"I've got something special," he said. "But I can't show you until we are inside."
Ben nodded and led the way to the secret room.

Donut looked around.

"Wow!" he said. "What a fantastic place!"

Mouse asked Donut what he had got for the secret room. Donut grinned and pulled off the sheet. There was a parrot, a real parrot in a cage.

"He's beautiful," murmured Sam as she stroked the parrot's feathers.

"But we've seen him before," complained Ben.

"We saw him when you moved in," Mouse added.

Duncan frowned. He had expected everyone to be really excited. Then a smile spread across his face.

"I know you've all seen Icarus before," he said. "But I bet you've never heard him."

Icarus looked at each of them, and he suddenly spoke in a high squawk. "I am not a Niggly Nagbag!" he screeched, sounding just like Cleo. Everyone laughed.

"He'll sit on my shoulder too." Donut boasted. Donut tried to put Icarus on his shoulder but the parrot had a better idea. Icarus wanted to fly round the room. He suddenly took off.

"Catch him!" shouted Donut. "Don't let him escape!"

Chapter Three

Escape!

The five children threw themselves at the parrot.
They jumped in the air.
They ran round the room.
They bumped into each other.
They fell over and sat on top
of each other.

They shouted and yelled,
while Icarus fluttered
just above them.

Donut crashed against the door. It swung wide open and out flew Icarus. The children scrambled out after him. They were just in time to see Icarus fly towards the sun.

Donut watched in despair. His face went white. "I am in big trouble now," he said. The others looked glum. There was nothing anyone could do.

"I'd better get back and tell Mum," muttered Donut, and he plodded home.

When Donut got home Cleo was waiting for him.
"You are a naughty boy," she said. "You are very very bad."
Donut had a sinking feeling inside. Everyone seemed to know that Icarus had escaped. What would he say to his parents?
He went into the front room and stared at the empty cage. He sat on a chair with his head in his hands.

Suddenly something banged against the window and Donut looked up. **Icarus!** The parrot was trying to get back in. He had flown home! Donut jumped up and opened the window. Icarus flew right into his cage. Donut let out a huge sigh. He was out of trouble!

Cleo pointed at him. "You are a naughty boy," she said again. "I am not a Niggly Nagbag!" She stopped and frowned at her brother. "Anyway, what is a Nagbag?"